IN THE
HOUSE
OF
HAPPINESS

A Book of Prayers and Praise

Selected by Neil Philip
Illustrated by Isabelle Brent

CLARION BOOKS
New York

FOR LESLIE, JOHN, AND LAURA BOLES
with love N.P.

FOR GEORGE AND BEV BUTLER
with love I.B.

Clarion Books
a Houghton Mifflin Company imprint
215 Park Avenue South
New York, NY 10003

Published in the United States in 2003 by arrangement with
The Albion Press Ltd, Spring Hill, Idbury, Oxfordshire OX7 6RU, England

Illustrations copyright © 2003 Isabelle Brent
Selection copyright © 2003 Neil Philip
For copyright of individual selections, see the acknowledgments
at the end of the book.
All rights reserved.

The illustrations were executed in watercolor and gold leaf.
The text was set in 12-point Weiss.

For information about permission to reproduce selections
from this book, write to Permissions, Houghton Mifflin Company,
215 Park Avenue South, New York, NY 10003.

www.houghtonmifflinbooks.com

Library of Congress Cataloging-in-Publication Data

In the house of happiness : a book of prayers and praise / selected by Neil Philip ; illustrated by
Isabelle Brent.
p. cm.
Summary: A collection of short prayers from major religions—Christianity, Judaism, Hinduism,
Buddhism, and Islam—along with tribal chants, folk rhymes, and poems of praise and devotion.
ISBN: 0-618-23481-0 (alk. paper)
[1. Children—Prayer books and devotions—English. 2. Prayer books and devotions.] I. Brent,
Isabelle, ill. II. Title.
BL625.5 .I65 2003
291.4/33 21   *2002010269*

Printed in China by Midas.

10 9 8 7 6 5 4 3 2 1

INTRODUCTION

The prayers in this book come from all over the world, and represent many faiths. Prayers of the great world religions—Christianity, Judaism, Hinduism, Buddhism, and Islam—mix with tribal chants, folk rhymes, and poems of praise and devotion.

They are divided into seven sections: "Bright Morning Stars Are Rising," "God's Praises," "Behold This Lovely World," "Simple Gifts," "What Can I Give?" "God Bless All Those That I Love," and "In the Great Night."

Many aspects of prayer are covered, from public praise to private meditation. But while the reasons for prayer are as varied as the human race, I was struck while compiling this book by how similar prayers from different cultures are. The instinct to pray seems deeply rooted in us, and the prayers of all religions express the same basic hopes, dreams, and fears.

In making the final choice from a much larger initial selection, I have had in mind the words of the great Jewish mystic Rabbi Nahman of Bratslav, who advised his followers to "pray in happiness, with a joyful tune."

Neil Philip

BRIGHT MORNING
STARS
ARE RISING

Bright morning stars are rising,
   Bright morning stars are rising,
   Bright morning stars are rising,
Day is a-breaking in my soul.

Oh, where are our dear fathers?
   Oh, where are our dear mothers?
Oh, where are our sisters and brothers?
   Day is a-breaking in my soul.

Some are down in the valley praying,
   Some are deep in the mountain sleeping,
Some are up in heaven shouting,
   Day is a-breaking in my soul.

AMERICAN *traditional*

This is the day which the Lord hath made; we will rejoice and be glad in it.

PSALM 118:24

The year's at the spring
And day's at the morn;
Morning's at seven;
The hillside's dew-pearled;
The lark's on the wing;
The snail's on the thorn:
God's in his heaven—
All's right with the world!

ROBERT BROWNING *English, 1812–89;*
from "Pippa Passes"

My God, the soul which you set within me is pure. You created it, you formed it, you breathed it into me, and you will preserve it within me. One day, you will reclaim it from me, but then you will restore it to me in the days to come.

As long as the soul is within me, I shall give thanks to you, Lord my God and God of my fathers, Master of all creation, Lord of all souls.

JEWISH *from the Talmud,*
translated by T. Carmi

Lord Jesus Christ, be with me today,
And help me in all I think, or do,
or say.

ENGLISH *traditional*

Protect me, O Lord;
My boat is so small,
And your sea is so big.

BRETON *traditional fisherman's prayer*

 A fragrant prayer upon the air
My child taught me,
Awaken there, the morn is fair,
The birds sing free.
Now dawns the day, awake and pray
And bend the knee,
The Lamb who lay beneath the clay
Was slain for thee.

BIDDY CRUMMY *Irish, 19th century*,
translated by Douglas Hyde

God be in my head
    and in my understanding;
    God be in my eyes
  and in my looking;
God be in my mouth and in my speaking;
God be in my heart and in my thinking;
God be at my end and at my departing.

ENGLISH *from the Sarum Primer,* 1527

The Architect of the world
    never does the same thing twice.
    Every day is an entirely new creation.
Take as much as you can from what each new
  day has to offer.

RABBI NAHMAN OF BRATSLAV 1772–1810,
translated by Moshe Mykoff

In the house of happiness,
 there I wander.
Beauty before me, with it I wander.
Beauty behind me, with it I wander.
Beauty below me, with it I wander.
Beauty above me, with it I wander.
Beauty all around me, with it I wander.
In old age traveling, with it I wander.
On the beautiful trail I am, with it I wander.

NATIVE AMERICAN *Navajo, from the Night Chant,*
translated by Washington Matthews;
"Song of Dawn Boy"

GOD'S PRAISES

Only a fool would fail
To praise God in his might
When the tiny mindless birds
Praise him in their flight.

IRISH *anonymous medieval monk*,
translated by Brendan Kennelly

Glory to God in the highest,
and on earth peace,
good will toward men.

ST. LUKE 2:14

In the beginning was God,
Today is God,
Tomorrow will be God.
Who can make an image of God?
He has no body.
He is the word which comes out
    of your mouth.
That word! It is no more,
It is past, and still it lives!
So is God.

AFRICAN *a Pygmy hymn*,
translated by John Mbiti

onor him, honor him
The revealed God.
His will is hard.
Say not: He is so high and far.
He rises up and floats down
And daily sees our deeds.
I am still young,
An inexperienced fool,
But day by day
I strive aloft toward wisdom's light.
Help me to bear the burden,
Show me life's revelation.

CHINESE *ancient prayer*

She, the eternal, was born in right olden times;
      She, the primeval, all things encompassed:
The great goddess, lighting up the dawn,
Looks out from each single thing that
      blinks the eye.

HINDU *from the Atharva-Veda*,
translated by R. C. Zaehner

O Goddess Laka!
      O wildwood bouquet, O Laka!
      O Laka, queen of the voice!
O Laka, giver of gifts!
O Laka, giver of bounty!
O Laka, giver of all things!

HAWAIIAN *prayer to Laka, goddess of the Hula*,
translated by Nathaniel B. Emerson

God is a God!
God don't never change!
God is a God
And he always will be God!

He made the sun to shine by day,
He made the sun to show the way,
He made the stars to show their light,
He made the moon to shine by night.

The earth his footstool, heaven his throne,
The whole creation all his own,
His love and power will prevail,
His promises will never fail.

God is a God!
God don't never change!
God is a God
And he always will be God!

AMERICAN *traditional spiritual*

When we assemble here
  to worship God,
   To sing his praises and
 to hear his word,
  We will walk softly.

With purity of heart, and with clean hands,
Our souls are free, we're free from
 Satan's bands,
  We will walk softly.

While we are passing through
 the sacred door,
Into the fold where Christ has gone before,
  We will walk softly.

We'll worship and bowed down
 we will rejoice,
And when we hear the shepherd's
 gentle voice
  We will walk softly.

AMERICAN *Shaker hymn*

BEHOLD THIS
LOVELY WORLD

Above, above
All birds in air

Below, below
All earth's flowers

Inland, inland
All forest trees

Seaward, seaward
All ocean fish

Sing out and say
Again the refrain

Behold this lovely world

MARY KAWENA PUKUI *Hawaiian, 1895–1986;*
"Behold"

O our Mother the Earth,
O our Father the Sky,
Your children are we, and
   with tired backs
We bring you the gifts that you love.
Then weave for us a garment of brightness;
May the warp be the white light of morning,
May the weft be the red light of evening,
May the fringes be the falling rain,
May the border be the standing rainbow.
Thus weave for us a garment of brightness
That we may walk fittingly where birds sing,
That we may walk fittingly
   where grass is green,
O our Mother the Earth,
   O our Father the Sky.

NATIVE AMERICAN *Tewa*,
translated by Herbert Joseph Spinden;
"Song of the Sky Loom"

The eye of the great God,
The eye of the God of glory,
The eye of the King of hosts,
The eye of the King of the living,

Pouring upon us
At each time and season,
Pouring upon us
Gently and generously.

Glory to thee,
Thou glorious sun.

Glory to thee, thou sun,
Face of the God of life.

SCOTTISH *traditional*,
translated by Alexander Carmichael

To touch the earth is a prayer.
To dig the earth is a prayer.
The dirt on my hands is sacred.
The light that falls on my face is sacred.
My prayer is my being.

NATIVE AMERICAN *Osage, from the Rite of Vigil,*
adapted from the translation by Francis La Flesche

The clear sky,
The green fruitful earth is good;
But peace among men is better.

NATIVE AMERICAN *Omaha,*
translated by Alice C. Fletcher

SIMPLE GIFTS

Thank you for the world so sweet,
Thank you for the food we eat.
Thank you for the birds that sing,
Thank you, God, for everything.

ENGLISH *traditional*

Some have meat and cannot eat,
Some cannot eat that want it:
But we have meat and we can eat,
So let the Lord be thankit.

ROBERT BURNS *Scottish, 1759–96*

O Lord,
Make us able
To eat all on the table.

ENGLISH *traditional*

Tis the gift to be simple,
'Tis the gift to be free,
'Tis the gift to come down
Where we ought to be.
And when we find ourselves
In the place just right,
'Twill be in the valley
Of love and delight.
When true simplicity is gained,
To bow and to bend we shan't be ashamed.
To turn, turn will be our delight,
'Til by turning, turning,
We come round right.

AMERICAN *Shaker hymn;*
"Simple Gifts"

Of all my gifts, I value most
        my life force.
    My feet, upon which I stand,
    I value.
My legs, with which I walk,
    I value.
My body, which gives me strength,
    I value.
My arms, which use my strength,
    I value.
My head, which contains my thoughts,
    I value.
My mouth, which speaks my thoughts,
    I value.
Of all my gifts, I value most
    my life force.

NATIVE AMERICAN *Osage, from the Rite of Vigil,*
adapted from the translation by Francis La Flesche

For walking here and there
   your feet are made.
For flying there are wings.
Your mouth is given you for speech.
And both your eyes to look on God.

INDIAN *traditional song of the Gonds,*
translated by Shamrao Hivale and Verrier Elwin

God, who created me
   Nimble and light of limb,
In three elements free,
   To run, to ride, to swim;
Not when the sense is dim,
   But now from the heart of joy,
I would remember him:
   Take the thanks of a boy.

HENRY CHARLES BEECHING *English, 1859–1919*

thou great Chief,
Light a candle in my heart,
That I may see what is therein,
And sweep the rubbish
from thy dwelling place.

AFRICAN *anonymous schoolgirl, 20th century*

 ere lie I, Martin Elginbrodde:
Have mercy on my soul, Lord God,
As I would do, were I Lord God
And you were Martin Elginbrodde.

SCOTTISH *epitaph in Elgin Cathedral*

I thank you, Lord, for knowing me
    better than I know myself,
  And for letting me know myself
better than others know me.
Make me, I ask you, then,
  better than others know me.
Make me, I ask you, then,
  better than they suppose,
And forgive me for what they do not know.

ABU BAKR *Muslim, 7th century*

Because I am poor,
  I pray
  For every living creature.

NATIVE AMERICAN *Kiowa,*
translated by James Mooney

WHAT CAN I GIVE?

In the bleak midwinter,
   Frosty wind made moan,
Earth stood hard as iron,
   Water like a stone;
Snow had fallen, snow on snow,
   Snow on snow,
In the bleak midwinter
   Long ago.

Our God, heaven cannot hold him,
   Nor earth sustain;
Heaven and earth shall flee away
   When he comes to reign:
In the bleak midwinter
   A stable-place sufficed
The Lord God Almighty,
   Jesus Christ.

What can I give him,
  Poor as I am?
If I were a shepherd,
  I would bring a lamb;
If I were a Wise Man,
  I would do my part—
Yet what I can, I give him:
  Give my heart.

CHRISTINA ROSSETTI *English, 1830–94;*
from "A Christmas Carol"

 It is more blessed
to give
than to receive.

ACTS 20:35

ake us worthy, Lord,
To serve our fellow men
Throughout the world
Who live and die
In poverty or hunger.
Give them, through our hands,
This day their daily bread,
And by our understanding love,
Give peace and joy.

MOTHER TERESA OF CALCUTTA *Macedonian,*
1910–1997

od, give us grace to accept with
serenity the things that cannot
be changed, courage to change
the things that should be changed, and
the wisdom to distinguish the one from
the other.

REINHOLD NIEBUHR *American, 1892–1971*

ord, make me an instrument
of your peace.
Where there is hatred,
let me sow love,
Where there is injury, pardon,
Where there is despair, hope,
Where there is darkness, light,
Where there is sadness, joy.

ST. FRANCIS OF ASSISI *Italian, 1181–1226*

 od give me work
Till my life shall end,
And life
Till my work be done.

ENGLISH *on the grave of the novelist*
Winifred Holtby, 1898–1935

GOD BLESS
ALL THOSE
THAT I LOVE

O God, make the door of this house wide enough to receive all who need human love and fellowship; narrow enough to shut out all envy, pride, and strife.

Make its threshold smooth enough to be no stumbling block to children, nor to straying feet, but rugged and strong enough to turn back the tempter's power.

God, make the door of this house the gateway to thine eternal kingdom.

BISHOP THOMAS KEN *English, 1637–1711*

God bless all those that I love,
God bless all those that love me.
God bless all those that love
those that I love, and those
that love those who love me.

AMERICAN *embroidered on a New England sampler*

Lord,
Keep my parents in your love.
Lord,
Bless them and keep them.
Lord,
Please let me have money and strength
And keep my parents for many more years
So that I can take care of them.

GHANAIAN *anonymous Christian, 20th century*

He prayeth best
Who loveth best
All things both
Great and small;
For the dear God
Who loveth us,
He made and loveth all.

SAMUEL TAYLOR COLERIDGE *English, 1772–1834;*
from "The Rime of the Ancient Mariner"

God bless us every one!

CHARLES DICKENS *English, 1812–70;*
Tiny Tim's prayer from *A Christmas Carol*

Gather up
In the arms of your pity
The sick, the depraved,
The desperate, the tired,
All the scum
Of our weary city
Gather up
In the arms of your pity.
Gather up
In the arms of your love—
Those who expect
No love from above.

LANGSTON HUGHES *American, 1902–67;*
"Prayer"

So long as we enjoy
    the light of day,
May we greet one another
 with love.
So long as we enjoy the
    light of day,
May we wish one another well.
Clasping hands,
Holding one another tight,
May we pray for each other:
    May you be blessed with light;
    May your roads be fulfilled;
    May you grow old;
    May you be lucky;
    May your roads stretch
    To join the life-giving road
        of your sun father;
    May your roads all be fulfilled.

NATIVE AMERICAN *Zuni, from Sayataca's Night Chant*,
adapted from the translation by Ruth L. Bunzel

ay Mary Virgin's Son himself
Be a generous lamp to you,
To guide you over
The great and awful ocean of eternity.

SCOTTISH *traditional*,
translated by Alexander Carmichael

ay the road rise up to meet you,
May the wind be always
     at your back,
May the sun shine warm
   upon your face,
The rain fall soft on your fields;
And until we meet again,
May God hold you in the palm of his hand.

IRISH *traditional*

IN THE
GREAT NIGHT

unset rays are going fast
Now the well-fought day is past,
Birds are flying to their nests
And the beasts of the wood are seeking rest,
As I kneel by my bed and pray
Thanking God for this happy day.

NANCY FRANKLIN HIGHAM *English, 1926–38;*
"Evening Song"

 ood night! Good night!
Far flies the light.
But still God's love
Shall shine above,
Making all bright.
Good night! Good night!

VICTOR HUGO *French, 1802–85*

tar light, star bright,
First star I see tonight,
I wish I may, I wish I might,
Have the wish I wish tonight.

AMERICAN *traditional*

 wish I didn't have freckles
        on my face.
    I wish that my stomach went in
  instead of out.
I wish that he would stand on top of the
  tallest building and shout,
"I love you, Amanda."

One more wish:
  I wish my name was Amanda.

JUDITH VIORST *American, b. 1931;*
"Bertha's Wish"

How shall I begin my song
In the blue night that is settling?
I will sit here and begin my song.

Brown owls come here in the blue evening,
They are hooting about,
They are shaking their wings and hooting.

In the great night my heart will go out;
Toward me the darkness comes rattling.
In the great night my heart will go out.

OWL WOMAN *Native American, Papago,
19th–20th century,* translated by Frances Densmore

May I and my spirit
live and rest in peace this night,
O my God.

TAHITIAN *traditional*

Matthew, Mark, Luke, and John,
Bless the bed that I lie on.
Before I lay me down to sleep,
I pray the Lord my soul to keep.
Four corners to my bed,
Four angels there are spread,
Two at the foot and two at the head,
And four to carry me when I'm dead.
I go by sea, I go by land,
The Lord made me with his right hand.
Should any danger come to me,
Sweet Jesus Christ deliver me.
He's the branch and I'm the flower,
Pray God send me a happy hour,
Not only me but those who are near
And dear to me, this night and evermore.
And should I die before I wake,
I pray the Lord my soul to take.

ENGLISH *traditional*

The day is past, the sun is set,
      And the white stars are in the sky;
   While the long grass with dew is wet,
   And through the air the bats now fly.

The lambs have now lain down to sleep,
   The birds have long since sought their nests;
The air is still; and dark, and deep
   On the hillside the old wood rests.

Yet of the dark I have no fear,
   But feel as safe as when 'tis light;
For I know God is with me there,
   And he will guard me through the night.

For God is by me when I pray,
   And when I close my eyes in sleep,
I know that he will with me stay,
   And will all night watch by me keep.

For he who rules the stars and sea,
    Who makes the grass and trees to grow,
Will look on a poor child like me,
    When on my knees I to him bow.

He holds all things in his right hand,
    The rich, the poor, the great, the small;
When we sleep, or sit, or stand,
    Is with us, for he loves us all.

THOMAS MILLER *Scottish, 1807–1874;*
"Evening"

e still, and know that I am God.

PSALM 46:10

ACKNOWLEDGMENTS

We thank the following copyright holders for permission to reprint individual selections, as listed below. Every effort has been made to trace copyright holders, and we will be pleased to correct any errors or omissions in future editions.

Atheneum Books for Young Readers, an imprint of Simon & Schuster Children's Publishing Division, for "Bertha's Wish" from Judith Viorst, If I Were in Charge of the World and Other Worries (New York: Atheneum, 1981), copyright © 1981 by Judith Viorst; Bonanza Books, a division of Randon House, Inc., for "God Is a God" from John W. Work, American Negro Songs and Spirituals (New York: Crown Publishers, 1940), copyright 1940, 1968 by Crown Publishers; David Campbell Publishers Ltd. for "She, the Eternal" from R. C. Zaehner, Hindu Scriptures (London: Everyman's Library, 1992), copyright © 1992 by David Campbell Publishers Ltd.; Friendship Press and the Church Missionary Society for "Lord, Keep My Parents in Your Love" from Morning, Noon, and Night, edited by Rev. John Carden; copyright © 1976 by Friendship Press; HarperCollins Publishers for "For Walking Here and There" from Shamrao Hivale and Verrier Elwin, Songs of the Forest: The Folk Poetry of the Gonds (London: George Allen & Unwin, 1935),copyright 1935 by Shamrao Hivale and Verrier Elwin; Jewish Lights Publishing, P.O. Box 237, Woodstock, VT 05091, www.jewishlights.com, for "The Architect of the World" from The Empty Chair: Finding Hope and Joy – Timeless Wisdom from a Hasidic Master, Rebbe Nachman of Breslov (Woodstock, VT: Jewish Lights Publishing, 1994), copyright © 1994 by the Breslov Research Institute; Alfred A. Knopf, a division of Random House, Inc. for "Prayer" from Langston Hughes, The Collected Poems of Langston Hughes, edited by Arnold Rampersad (New York: Alfred A. Knopf, 1994), copyright © 1994 by the Estate of Langston Hughes; Elisabeth Sifton for "God, Give Us Grace to Accept with Serenity" from Reinhold Niebuhr, Justice and Mercy, edited by Ursula M. Niebuhr (New York: Harper & Row, 1974), copyright © 1974 by Ursula M. Niebuhr; Oxford University Press for "O Thou Great Chief" from George Appleton, The Oxford Book of Prayer (Oxford and New York: Oxford University Press, 1985); Penguin Books for "Thanksgiving Upon Awakening" ("My God, the soul which you set within me is pure") from T. Carmi, The Penguin Book of Hebrew Verse (New York: Viking, and London: Allen Lane, 1981), copyright © 1981 by T. Carmi, and for "God's Praises" ("Only a fool would fail") from Brendan Kennelly, The Penguin Book of Irish Verse (Harmondsworth: Penguin, 1981), copyright © 1970, 1981 by Brendan Kennelly; Neil Philip for the Introduction and adaptations of "To Touch the Earth Is a Prayer," "Of All My Gifts," and "So Long As We Enjoy the Light of Day," copyright © 2003 by Neil Philip; the Society for Promoting Christian Knowledge for "In the Beginning Was God" from Professor John Mbiti, Prayers of African Religion (London: Society for Promoting Christian Knowledge, 1975), copyright © 1975 by the Society for Promoting Christian Knowledge; the University Press of Hawaii for "Behold" from The Echo of Our Song: Chants and Poems of the Hawaiians, translated and edited by Mary K. Pukui and Alfons L. Korn (Honolulu: University Press of Hawaii, 1973), copyright © 1973 by the University Press of Hawaii; "Evening Song" is reprinted from Nancy Franklin Higham, Verses (privately printed, 1939); "Honor Him, Honor Him, the Revealed God" is reprinted from A. C. Bouquet, Sacred Books of the World (Harmondsworth: Penguin, 1954); all rights in respect of the Authorized King James Version of the Holy Bible, 1662, are vested in the Crown in the United Kingdom and controlled by Royal Letters Patent.

For Kevin and Casey, my nephews.